ESOL and citizenship

A teachers' guide

Chris Taylor

niace

promoting adult learning

promoting adult learning

© 2007 National Institute of
(England and Wales)

21 De Montfort Street
Leicester LE1 7GE

Company registration no. 2603322
Charity registration no. 1002775

NIACE has a broad remit to promote lifelong learning opportunities for
adults. NIACE works to develop increased participation in education
and training, particularly for those who do not have easy access
because of class, gender, age, race, language and culture, learning
difficulties or disabilities, or insufficient financial resources.

You can find NIACE online at **www.niace.org.uk**

Cover design by Creative, Langbank, Scotland
Designed and typeset by Creative, Langbank, Scotland
Printed and bound by Ashford Colour Press Ltd

Contents

Foreword v

Mary Coussey, Chair, Advisory Board on Naturalisation and Integration

Introduction vi

Chapter 1: Background...1
  The policy background 1
  Citizenship in schools..4
  Post-16 citizenship 5
  New developments – the test for settlement.........................6

Chapter 2: Applying for citizenship 9
  The application process 9
  The Life in the UK test 10
  The launch of the test..11
  Sample questions...13
  The citizenship ceremony 15
  The benefits of citizenship 18

Chapter 3: Definitions of citizenship......................................21
  Introduction..21
  What is citizenship?...22
  Citizenship as a legal status 23
  Citizenship as feeling – identity 23
  Citizenship in practice...25
  Implications for the ESOL classroom...................................26

Chapter 4: The ESOL citizenship project 29
  Introduction..29
  Issues...31
  Feedback from teachers and learners 33
  Who knows more?...34

As good as the teacher 35
Going local 35
The teachers' views 35

Chapter 5: Learning activities 39
Introduction 39
What is citizenship? 40
Parliament and the electoral system 41
UK geography and history 43
The UK as a diverse society 47
Community engagement – volunteering 50
Human rights 52

Chapter 6: ESOL and citizenship provision 55
Introduction 55
Model 1: Citizenship integrated in all provision 55
Model 2: ESOL and citizenship as separate provision 56
Model 3: ESOL and citizenship module 56
Model 4: Prepare for the test 57
Implications and issues 58
Accreditation and evidence for inspection 60
A checklist to choose the topics 60
Case studies 63

References and resources 69
Home Office regulations and citizenship 69
Citizenship for ESOL learners – learning materials 71

Foreword

The new naturalisation procedures which came into effect in November 2005 require that applicants have a certain level of English language and knowledge of life in the UK. Those whose language levels are below English for Speakers of Other Languages (ESOL) Entry Level 3 (Access Level in Scotland) can meet these requirements by gaining an ESOL qualification, based on the *Citizenship Materials for ESOL Learners* prepared by the National Institute of Adult Continuing Education (NIACE) and LLU+.

The author of this book was one of the key architects of those materials. She was involved in developing the learning materials with ESOL providers in the pilot process and in disseminating knowledge about these materials in workshops with ESOL teachers throughout the UK. This book draws on her unique and wide experience. It contains information about the naturalisation requirements and useful background information on the context, including facts on immigration which can be used to dispel some of the common myths. It contains examples of the teaching models and learning activities with comments from the learners and from teachers.

This book is timely and provides an authoritative insight into ESOL and citizenship. It brings the materials alive with examples which have been particularly valued by learners.

The underlying aim of the new naturalisation requirements is to encourage integration. By improving language skills and knowledge of life in the UK, immigrants have a better basis for being actively involved in work and in social interaction with settled residents. The experiences and activities on which this book is based will help with the integration process. Participative activities are an important tool for integration, regardless of whether the learners are applicants for naturalisation.

I welcome this book and I am sure that it will be a rich source of information.

Mary Coussey, Chair, Advisory Board on Naturalisation and Integration

Introduction

Since November 2005, everyone who wishes to apply to become a UK citizen has to prove they have a certain level of English language and some knowledge of the United Kingdom. They can do this in one of two ways. They can either take an online citizenship test – the *Life in the UK* test – or they can gain a qualification in English language. This book explains that process and puts the new regulations in the policy context. It also gives practical ideas for teaching English language through citizenship.

This book comes from a three-year project on English for speakers of other languages (ESOL) and citizenship, led by the National Institute of Adult Continuing Education (NIACE) and LLU+, and funded by the Home Office and the Department for Education and Skills (DfES). The book draws on the project findings and the pilot process, developing learning materials with ESOL providers.

Who the book is for

ESOL teachers

This book is for all ESOL teachers working in England, Scotland, Northern Ireland and Wales, in further education colleges, in adult and community learning, in the voluntary sector or in private training providers. Although it is a book about a specialist subject – the language a learner needs to apply for UK citizenship – it will be useful because ESOL teachers are all, in some way, also advisers to learners. For ESOL learners, the first point of contact for information and advice is often the ESOL teacher. It is important to know about the significant changes to the legal requirements for naturalisation and settlement. The book will explain the Home Office language requirements and suggest ways in which citizenship learning materials can be adapted for different learners at Entry Level (Access Level in Scotland).

ESOL managers

If you are an ESOL manager, you will want to consider if you should be offering ESOL and citizenship courses as part of your provision and how to integrate the new courses into existing provision. The book will describe different models of provision and give case studies of stand-alone 'Prepare for the Test' courses, separate ESOL and citizenship courses and fully-integrated ESOL provision where citizenship is an element of all courses. You will find most of the book useful, but particularly Chapter 6 on different types of provision.

Student advisers and learning advisers

Student advisers are a vital source of information to potential learners and in the area of ESOL and citizenship it is essential to get it right. It is a fine line between the learner at Entry Level 3 (Intermediate 3 in Scotland) who could easily pass the Life in the UK Test, and the learner working towards Entry Level 3 who needs a one-year *Skills for Life* ESOL course. You will find this book useful in advising learners about the language requirements for UK settlement and citizenship. You will also find the information you need in helping the learner make an informed choice about learning. For learners at borderline Entry Level 3/Level 1 (Intermediate 3 in Scotland), it is not a straightforward decision. If they wish to apply for citizenship, they must choose either one year studying ESOL at Entry Level to achieve a *Skills for Life* qualification in speaking and listening or taking the 45-minute online test, *Life in the UK*, costing £34. You will find Chapters 1, 2 and 4 most useful and relevant but, hopefully, you will find the rest of the book interesting too.

Voluntary sector advisers

If you work in the voluntary sector, you will find this book accessible and useful. The key information you need in advising individuals is in Chapters 1 and 2 and the section on references and resources should help to give the bigger picture. You may also choose Chapter 6 on types of provision. As the *Life in the UK Test*, or citizenship test, is better established, many voluntary sector providers or private agencies are offering 'Prepare for the Test' types of courses. You may wish to offer such a course yourselves, but you will certainly want to give the community you serve the best possible advice.

This book will:

- give information on applying for UK citizenship;
- examine the background to the introduction of citizenship for ESOL learners;
- put in context the recent media coverage of immigration and citizenship;
- suggest learning activities for ESOL and citizenship; and
- describe models of provision.

Chapter 1
Background

The policy background

In 2002, the government announced its intention to make becoming a British citizen a more meaningful event. The then Home Secretary, David Blunkett, set up an advisory group chaired by Sir Bernard Crick 'to consider how best to achieve the government's plans to promote language skills and practical knowledge about the United Kingdom for those seeking to become British citizens'. *The New and the Old*, the Advisory Group's report, was published in 2003. The report proposed a wide-ranging set of recommendations for immigrants wishing to apply for UK citizenship. These included a handbook about living in the UK to be given to all immigrants, an entitlement to language provision on arrival, a ceremony to celebrate the acquisition of citizenship and the introduction of a new citizenship test. The report also included some flexible and innovative ideas on routes to citizenship, such as demonstration of progression in language rather than one fixed language standard, as well as mentoring and community involvement. The Group made specific suggestions on what a programme of citizenship study should include and identified six key areas:

- Britain as a diverse society
- The law
- Employment
- British national institutions
- Sources of help and information
- Everyday needs

It stressed that the programme of study should be flexible, learner-centred and focused on speaking and listening.

The New and the Old report can be read against a background of policy on immigration, citizenship and community cohesion. In 2001, when Britain's worst race riots for twenty years took place in Bradford, Burnley and Oldham, the government began to develop a strategy to improve community cohesion. Herman Ouseley's report on community relations in Bradford described a city fragmented, with religious and ethnic communities segregated. But as soon as

Declaration of war on asylum

Send these scroungers home now

Still at large here, 126,000 asylum cheats

Asylum seekers in Scotland get cash handouts

community cohesion came to the top of the headlines, reporting on asylum-seekers and refugees became particularly hostile:

Tony Blair promised to cut the number of refugees to Britain by half and there was even consideration of withdrawing from the 1952 Geneva Convention and the European Convention on Human Rights.

So an interesting contradiction arose. The government pursued a punitive and unwelcoming approach to immigration, including our obligations to offer asylum, but at the same time introduced a liberal and inclusive approach to settlement and citizenship. The concept of community cohesion, arising out of the 2001 riots, sits uneasily alongside the tensions which developed from contradictory government policies and practice. The 100,000 annual applicants for British citizenship can choose one of two routes to demonstrate their English language skills and citizenship knowledge. However, there are not enough ESOL courses and these applicants may remain for years on waiting lists as demand continues to exceed supply.

The government accepted the recommendation in the Crick report, that would-be citizens could demonstrate that they had made progress in ESOL by achieving an Entry Level qualification in speaking and listening (or two ESOL units at Access Level in Scotland). At the same time, Sir Bernard Crick acknowledged that there were neither enough ESOL courses nor enough ESOL teachers to meet existing demand. One of the members of the Advisory Group, Annette Zera, said:

> *It's a matter of human rights. If you are not able to speak, read or write the language of the country you live in, you cannot exercise your full rights as a citizen and are likely to be excluded and exploited.*
>
> (*Times Education Supplement*, 3 September 2004)

The government also demonstrated that it was aware of the significant contribution that immigrants made to the UK economy, but this did not hit the newspaper headlines in the same way. The Institute for Public Policy Research report published in April 2005 showed that migrants were paying disproportionately more tax than would be expected for their share of the population.

> *When the budget is in the black, migrant workers put in more than UK-born workers – when the budget is in the red, they take out less than UK-born workers.*
>
> (Danny Sriskandarajah, Senior Research Fellow, IPPR)

In July 2006, while questioning Tony Blair, the House of Commons Select Committee identified 'the confusion amongst ... ministers about what we are trying to do about British citizenship'. Mr Blair referred to migration, which he said was 'the biggest issue on the agenda of most European countries' and he was asked what makes a good citizen.

> *I think the most important thing is that everybody who comes into this country shares the basic values of the country, values about democracy, the rule of law and tolerance and respect for people of other faiths and races and creeds. I think that is the most important thing. What binds us together and makes us British are the common values we have.*
>
> (Evidence of the Prime Minister to the Chairs of the Commons Select Committee, 4 July 2006)

Gordon Brown acknowledged the benefits to the British economy from migrants in an interview with the *Today* programme on BBC Radio 4 but said that people should learn English, understand British history and 'play by the rules'.

> *I think people who come into this country, who are part of our community, should play by the rules. I think learning English is part of that. That's why I want to see changes in the curriculum. I would insist on [sic] large numbers of people who have refused to learn our language that they must do so.*
>
> (Gordon Brown, BBC Radio 4 *Today* programme, 5 June 2006)

Citizenship in schools

The report of the 'Life in the United Kingdom' Advisory Group did not stand in isolation. The Chair, Sir Bernard Crick, had already advised the government on the citizenship agenda for schools and from September 2002 there was a statutory requirement for schools to include it in the curriculum. Citizenship is now part of the national curriculum in primary and secondary schools. The three key aspects are social and moral responsibility, community involvement and political literacy.

> *Citizenship is more than a statutory subject. If taught well and tailored to local needs, its skills and values will enhance democratic life for us all, both rights and responsibilities, beginning in school and radiating out.*
>
> (Sir Bernard Crick, Birkbeck College, London)

The model of citizenship education 'radiating out' was also favoured by David Blunkett who recommended starting with the local neighbourhood, radiating out to the national and global issues.

At Key Stages 1 and 2, citizenship is part of the non-statutory framework for Personal, Social and Health Education (PSHE) and Citizenship. At Key Stages 3 and 4, Citizenship is a new foundation subject in the National Curriculum.

However, in January 2005 a survey showed that the schools' citizenship curriculum was not as effective as had been hoped. The ICM poll showed that one in ten pupils did not know what a citizenship class was and 17 per cent said there was nothing memorable about it. Only 25 per cent of teenagers knew that Labour was in government.

There is an interesting contrast here with the knowledge required to pass the new citizenship test. New citizens must pass the test by learning key chapters from the Home Office handbook, *Life in the United Kingdom: A Journey to Citizenship*. The chapters cover migration to Britain, the changing role of women, families, population, religion and tolerance, the regions of Britain, customs and traditions, government, formal institutions, the devolved administrations, Britain in Europe and the world and the ordinary citizen. By this measure, it seems likely that new citizens will be more knowledgeable about the UK than citizens born here.

Post-16 citizenship

The post-16 citizenship development programme, led by the Learning and Skills Development Agency (LSDA), was set up in 2001 and offered materials and training to organisations delivering citizenship teaching to young people.

The programme produced learning materials such as:

- College politics: a role-playing game from Richmond-upon-Thames College
- What is active citizenship?
- Cultural diversity table – devised by Whalley Range High School

and also assessment materials such as:

- Are you a political animal? A magazine quiz by Merton College and case studies such as:

- Running a mock parliamentary election – a case study and activity from Camden Job Train
- Raising awareness of multicultural life in Leicester – William Bradford Community College

The programme encouraged young learners to gain the knowledge, understanding and skills required to play an effective role in society.

From September 2006 a new support programme was taken forward by the Learning and Skills Network, building on the LSDA's work. The website is a useful resource for teachers working with young people: www.post16citizenship.org

New developments – the test for settlement

The Home Office five-year strategy for asylum and immigration was announced by the Home Secretary, Charles Clarke, in February 2005, and introduced a new points system for migration. A four-tier points system was introduced:

- Tier One – highly-skilled workers, including doctors and engineers
- Tier Two – skilled workers, including teachers and nurses
- Tier Three – low-skilled workers including agricultural workers and those in the hospitality industry
- Tier Four – students

Only skilled migrant workers in Tiers One and Two would be allowed to settle in the UK after five years, and only if they passed the Life in the UK test and satisfied the English language requirement. So, applicants for settlement would then be in a similar position to applicants for citizenship. They would have to pass the *Life in the UK* test or follow an ESOL with Citizenship course. Unskilled and low-skilled migrant workers and students would have no right to settle in the UK at all. Low-skilled workers would be barred from citizenship and would be expected to leave the UK after five years.

This strategy is likely to increase the demand for ESOL courses and ESOL and Citizenship courses. There will be a continuing tension between the requirement to obtain an ESOL qualification and difficulty in securing a place on a course.

Referring to the German system of 'guest workers', critics warned against creating a 'Gastarbeiter economy' with low-skilled workers enjoying fewer rights than other migrants. The strategy, *Controlling our Borders: Making Migration Work for Britain,* introduced further measures to increase detention, make refugee status only a temporary leave to remain and introduce ID cards for foreign nationals, among others. This sharpened the contrast between the government's strict immigration policy and a more liberal approach to citizenship acquisition.

Learners at the Chinese Centre (North of England)

Chapter 2

Applying for citizenship

The application process

It is now possible to apply for UK citizenship in two ways. Applicants must be over 18 and must have lived in the UK for five years (they cannot have been away from the country for more than 90 days in the last year, or 450 days in the last five years). If married to a UK citizen, they must have lived in the UK for three years and not have been out of the country for more than 270 days in the three years. They also have to be of 'good character', which means that they have to have a clean police record.

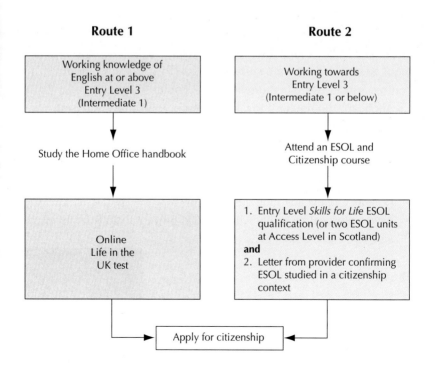

Route 1	Route 2
Working knowledge of English at or above Entry Level 3 (Intermediate 1)	Working towards Entry Level 3 (Intermediate 1 or below)
↓	↓
Study the Home Office handbook	Attend an ESOL and Citizenship course
↓	↓
Online Life in the UK test	1. Entry Level *Skills for Life* ESOL qualification (or two ESOL units at Access Level in Scotland) **and** 2. Letter from provider confirming ESOL studied in a citizenship context

Apply for citizenship

They also have to demonstrate competence in the English language and knowledge of life in the UK. This can be done in one of two ways:

To demonstrate their language skills and knowledge of life in the UK, applicants can take the new online citizenship test, called the *Life in the UK Test*. This is designed for those who have English language skills at Entry Level 3 (Intermediate 1 in Scotland) or above, the majority of citizenship applicants.

There is plenty of additional information on the test website (www.lifeintheuktest.gov.uk), including a few sample questions.

If they cannot understand the tutorial on the website, then applicants probably need to enrol on an ESOL and citizenship course.

The alternative route, if they have English language skills at Entry Level 3 (Intermediate 1 in Scotland) or below, is to follow an ESOL and citizenship course and achieve a *Skills for Life* qualification in speaking and listening. The Home Office requires that the ESOL course must include some of the learning materials from *Citizenship Materials for ESOL learners*, the pack published by NIACE (see: www.esolcitizenship.org.uk). So, for those with English language skills below Entry Level 3, the focus is on learning English and they are not required to take a separate citizenship test. The ESOL citizenship courses are discussed in more detail in Chapter 4.

Applicants do not have to take the test or follow an ESOL and citizenship course if they:

- are over 65;
- have a long-term health condition;
- have a cognitive learning difficulty; or
- have a physical disability which would prevent them from going to an ESOL class or taking the test.

The Life in the UK test

Applicants can take the citizenship test on a computer at one of the *Life in the UK* test centres. It consists of 24 questions. Forty-five minutes are allowed for the test, but most

people complete it in less. The test can be taken as many times as required.

The test is based on the handbook *Life in the UK: A Journey to Citizenship* – Chapters 2–6. The handbook is available in hard copy, priced £9.99, from The Stationery Office (TSO) and can be ordered by telephone on 0870 243 0123, or online at www.tso.co.uk/bookshop.

Further details about the test are at: www.lifeintheuktest.gov.uk. This website also contains a full list of centres where the test can be taken; applicants simply type in their home postcode. Or they can call the Life in the UK test helpline on 0800 015 4245.

If applicants pass the test they will *not* need to produce additional proof of their knowledge of English.

They will need to take a passport or photographic driving licence to the test centre. Alternatively, applicants can take a passport-sized photo, signed on the back by a professional person who knows them. The photo will then be signed by a member of the test centre staff and forwarded to the Home Office. The test costs £34 and applicants will be told the result on the same day. They will get a pass notification letter, which needs to be kept safe and attached to the completed citizenship application form when applying to the Home Office. The test centre also notifies the Home Office of all results.

The launch of the test

The government's launch of the *Life in the UK* test in November 2005 provoked a media response, nationally and internationally. The Immigration Minister, Tony McNulty, said at the launch:

> *This is not a test of someone's ability to be British or a test of their Britishness. It is a test of their preparedness to become citizens, in keeping with the language requirement as well.*
>
> (Tony McNulty, speech at the launch hosted by Advisory Board for Naturalisation and Integration, 1 November 2005)

But the press had a field day and criticised the test for being too easy or too difficult. The *Washington Post's* article *'It's hard to be British'* reflected:

> *British commentators have poked fun at the test, wondering how many native-born citizens would know some of the more arcane information the new comers were being asked to learn – that about 25% of British children live in single parent homes, for instance, and that women and initially only those over 30, won the right to vote in 1918.*
>
> (Washington Post, 1 November 2005)

The Russian newspaper *Pravda* put the test in a political context. The test 'is only part of the solution to easing immigration tensions in the United Kingdom, where fear of immigrants has intensified since the September 11th 2001 attacks in the United States and the bombings in Madrid and London'.

The *Daily Mail* was one of the government's fiercest critics even before the test was launched. There were rumours about the content of the test. Then their headline read:

> *Learn to claim benefits and complain about the police ... but you don't need to know who this famous Briton was.*
>
> (*Daily Mail*, 16 June 2005)

Although this particular article was inaccurate, the general tone of disapproval prevailed in the popular press. Other comments were more measured but still critical. The Shadow Home Secretary David Davies welcomed the test, but said it

© EMPICS

was 'a disgrace that the sample questions seem to show there will be nothing about history in the test'.

Other commentators picked up on the contradiction. The Immigration Advisory Service (IAS) gave the test a cautious welcome but feared that 'this will be a way of excluding people from British citizenship' (Keith Best, Chief Executive IAS, November 2005). Trevor Phillips, chairman of the Commission for Racial Equality, told BBC radio that he was opposed to a test but said that immigrants should be encouraged to develop skills to integrate into society.

Some newspapers published the sample test questions released by the Home Office as part of the launch, but others like BBC News online took the *Life in the UK* handbook and compiled their own questions. The BBC also set up a website where readers could suggest questions for new citizens, some for fun and some which would defeat most readers!

1. The consumption of which dish will most impress your drunken British colleagues?
   - Chicken tikka masala
   - Chicken vindaloo
   - Chicken phal

2. Describe the difference between the United Kingdom, Great Britain and the British Isles.

Sample questions

There are four types of question in the online test. The first type is multiple choice, where one answer is selected from four options. For example:

1) Which one of these courts uses a jury system?
   - Magistrates' court
   - Crown court
   - Youth court
   - County court

2) How old do you have to be to buy alcohol?
   * 14
   * 16
   * 18
   * 21

3) Who appoints Life Peers to the House of Lords?
   * The Speaker of the House of Commons
   * The Leader of the House of Lords
   * The Prime Minister
   * The Lord Chancellor

The second type of question is "true or false". For example:

Is the statement below true or false?
   Your employer can dismiss you for joining a trade union.
   * True
   * False

The next type involves selecting two correct answers from four options. For example:

   Which two telephone numbers can be used to dial the emergency services?
   * 112
   * 123
   * 555
   * 999

The last question type asks which one of two statements is correct. For example:

   Which one of these two statements is correct?
   * A television licence is required for each television in a home
   * A single television licence covers all televisions in a home

The citizenship ceremony

Once applicants have successfully taken the test or completed a course, to become a citizen they must attend a citizenship ceremony and take an Oath and Pledge to the United Kingdom. The Home Office writes to invite the applicant to a ceremony if the application is successful. They will send the wording of the Oath and Pledge and the phone number and address of the local authority. Then the applicant must contact the local authority to book the ceremony.

Citizenship ceremonies are normally organised by:

- local councils in England, Scotland and Wales; and
- the Northern Ireland Office.

On arrival at the ceremony, there is usually a group of other new citizens. The Registrar hosts the ceremony. The applicant must show the invitation and then receives a card with the words that have to be said. After a welcome speech, the Registrar invites all the applicants to take the Oath or the Affirmation. Each applicant can choose to take an Oath:

'I swear by Almighty God ...'

or choose the Affirmation,

'I do solemnly and sincerely affirm...'

After the Oath or Affirmation, applicants take the Citizenship Pledge:

'I will give my loyalty to the United Kingdom and respect its rights and freedoms.

I will uphold its democratic values.

I will observe its laws faithfully and fulfil my duties and obligations as a British citizen.'

Then they receive the citizenship certificate and an information pack. After the citizenship ceremony the local authority will tell the Home Office who has attended and then all the applicants are free to apply for a British passport.

Children cannot be included in a citizenship certificate but they can be considered for registration as British citizens too. When applicants complete the application form, they can give their children's details too.

Children who are part of a family application also receive invitations to the citizenship ceremony but they do not take the Oath. At the ceremony, they will simply be given their citizenship certificates. Parents receive the certificate of children who cannot attend.

The first ceremony took place in February 2004 in Brent, North West London. The *Guardian* interviewed a sample of new citizens at a ceremony in Brent in November 2004. According to the paper, the ceremony achieved a balance between solemnity and informality. The 16 interviewees came from countries colonised by Britain, such as South Africa or New Zealand, or countries in conflict, like Somalia or

Prince Charles presents a certificate to a new citizen at the first citizenship ceremony in Brent

Iraq. Mohamed Jubber from Iraq, who fled Saddam Hussein's regime, said 'Iraq is a bit difficult now. We hope to stay in Britain because we love this country. We enjoy our life here'. Rohana and Sharmalie Ranasinghe from Sri Lanka applied for British citizenship because their three daughters were British and for the convenience of foreign travel with a UK passport. They described their daughters: 'they think like British people'.

All the new citizens interviewed gave positive feedback about the citizenship ceremony experience, just as David Blunkett had described the event he attended in July 2004 as Home Secretary:

> *...I came away with a real sense that this was a powerful way of boosting personal, civic and national pride, challenging society to offer a welcome to those who have positively chosen to take our nationality.*

(Extract from a speech, 7 July 2004)

New citizens with the mayor and registrar at a citizenship ceremony in Brent

New citizens in Brent display their certificates

The benefits of citizenship

With UK citizenship, it is possible to apply for a British passport and use this to travel. Refugees who fled their home country without documents or whose passports have since expired find this particularly useful. Even if an applicant is already a citizen of another country, they may wish to apply for British citizenship because it may give more freedom to travel. For example, certain countries may require visas if the individual uses their original passport, so where a British passport does not require a visa, they could use a British passport instead.

There is no restriction on a British national being a citizen of another country as well. So, it is not necessary to give up any other nationality when becoming a UK citizen. Many other countries, however, do not allow dual nationality so an individual may, as a naturalised British citizen, lose their existing nationality.

UK citizens can work anywhere in the EU, stand for election as a local councillor, Member of Parliament (MP) or Member of the

European Parliament (MEP) and vote in a local election, general election or European election. (Commonwealth citizens and Irish citizens have all these rights anyway. EU citizens can vote in local or European elections only; they can stand as candidates too.)

Chapter 3
Definitions of citizenship

Introduction

This chapter will discuss the concept of citizenship, what it feels to be a citizen and how that works out in daily life. It asks, what does it take to feel British? Does Norman Tebbit's infamous cricket test have any relevance? The notions of a 'good' citizen and an 'active' citizen and then the implications for teaching ESOL and citizenship are considered. Are ESOL teachers helping learners to become British citizens or encouraging them to be active citizens living in Britain? The following definitions of citizenship appeared on the website www.answers.com

The status of a citizen, with its attendant duties, rights and privileges

The quality of an individual's behaviour as a citizen

Membership of a political community

Largely co-terminous with nationality

During the pilot of the *Citizenship Materials for ESOL Learners* pack, teachers struggled with the definition of citizenship and untangling the teaching of language, which was the primary purpose, and the teaching of citizenship. A similar confusion was identified by Sir Bernard Crick in the teaching of citizenship in schools, regarding the two senses of citizenship – the legal and the political. Perhaps this is partly why the Chief Inspector of Schools, David Bell, said that headteachers and senior managers 'misunderstood and undervalued' citizenship as a subject (*Guardian*, 2 November 2005).

New citizens with Princess Anne at a citizenship ceremony

What is citizenship?

Citizenship is most often understood as status. The legal status of a citizen is currently determined as relating to a particular nation state. Political debates and policy development focus on who is, and who is not, a citizen, with particular rights and obligations. In this sense, citizenship is exclusive, since there is a clear-cut distinction between those who have this status and those who do not. Yet citizenship is much more than status, it also involves feeling, the degree to which individuals feel they belong, and citizenship participation and engagement, which can be termed the practice of citizenship.

(Osler and Starkey, 2005)

This useful description of three aspects of citizenship can inform ESOL classroom practice.

Citizenship as a legal status

ESOL teachers are asked to teach ESOL and citizenship courses to help applicants apply for naturalisation. The courses have an extrinsic purpose as part of the process, described in the previous chapter. But does learning a language in the context of citizenship also have an intrinsic value? Evidence from the trial of the ESOL citizenship materials suggested that it does and that learners valued learning about the UK for its own sake.

> *Because I live in the UK I should know everything about this country, for example, citizenship is very important and I need passport and also about law and services.*
>
> (Sheffield College learner)

The implications for classroom practice will be further discussed later in this chapter.

Citizenship as feeling – identity

Separating out the two notions of becoming British or becoming a citizen in Britain is helpful here. By becoming British, we do not mean applying for naturalisation but, rather, being like the British. This is presumably where Norman Tebbit's 'cricket test' applies. The cricket test was a phrase used by Tebbit in referring to the loyalties of immigrants to the UK in the 1990s. The Conservative politician, in an interview with the *Los Angeles Times*, said:

> *A large proportion of Britain's Asian population fail to pass the cricket test. Which side do they cheer for? It's an interesting test. Are you still harking back to where you came from or where you are?*

Sharmalie Ranasinghe, quoted in Chapter 2, at the citizenship ceremony in Brent described his experience of this dichotomy regarding feelings of nationalism. He and his wife are from Sri Lanka but he said his daughters, born in the UK, 'think like British people'. But what does it mean to be typically British? Many commentators cite the values of democracy, fair play and supporting the underdog as typically British. Tony Blair talked about the British 'tolerance and respect for people of other faiths and races and creeds' (Evidence to All Commons Select Committee, 4 July 2006).

But others have pointed out that these are values shared by citizens of many other countries and are characteristics that other countries would use to describe themselves. They are not distinctly British.

Which features of Britain are 'typically' British? Typical Britishness is, in fact, both multi-faceted and fluid. It is an evolving concept. Some years ago the British way of life did not include Chinese takeaways, Pakistani doctors or Indian shopkeepers. It did not include Sunday trading (now so much changed that shopping has become the Sunday leisure activity). It is often said to include fish and chips, described as typically British on the government-sponsored website, *Icons: A Portrait of England*. But fish and chips is an imported dish brought over by Huguenot immigrants in the seventeenth century. What could be more typically British than tea drinking? Yet most urban landscapes are today littered with coffee shops. The typically British way of life has changed over time and it is different depending on where in Britain you live. For example, in London it is unusual to queue for a bus or to thank the driver as you get off; in other parts of the UK it is customary.

Sarfraz Mansoor, writing in *The Observer*, quotes the judge who described binge drinkers as 'simply savages, angry, blind and brutal... they are so ill-educated or made crude by inadequately civilizing influences in their homes' (*The Observer*, 21 August 2005). Is this part of being British? Mansoor also cites his own experience as a child of immigrants, when the most hurtful insult was 'Go back home', since he was already home and the words implied he did not belong in Britain.

Nevertheless, there are clearly cross-cultural differences which are noticed by any newcomer to Britain. The recent series of HSBC bank adverts on television showed examples of cross-cultural misunderstandings in different countries and the consequences of getting it wrong. For example, a biker is shown on his travels in South America where the forefinger-to-thumb gesture, 'OK', signifies approval. In Brazil, it is considered rude. 'We never underestimate the importance of local knowledge' (HSBC). Newcomers to Britain are perhaps the people best qualified to identify what they consider to be typically British as cultural differences appear in stark contrast to customs at home.

Citizenship in practice

Sir Bernard Crick explains that the difference between being a good citizen and being an active citizen is elementary. You can be a good citizen in an autocratic state but you may face penalties if you are an active citizen; for example, by joining a protest demonstration or organising a community group. In a democracy, you can be a good citizen by voting and obeying the law but this is passive citizenship. You can, in addition, be an active citizen by contributing to your local community, being a parent governor at the local school, running a youth group or setting up a supplementary school.

The notion of active citizenship links with the school citizenship curriculum, encouraging young people to be assertive, to contribute to society and to become involved in the local community. Some refugees have past experience of being active citizens in their home country. Indeed, it may be the reason for their persecution and exile.

The government's community cohesion strategy pivots on the active engagement of people with their local communities and becoming active citizens in a very practical way. When individuals are active citizens they are more inclined to feel themselves stakeholders in a community and of course the reverse is also true. When individuals feel they are stakeholders, they wish to invest in the local community and, by contributing to it, become active citizens. It is only when the majority feel they are stakeholders that community cohesion is achieved. Community cohesion is not achieved once and for all but is a feeling and something that has to be developed continually.

Implications for the ESOL classroom

ESOL teachers taking part in the pilot of learning materials raised a number of concerns about teaching ESOL in the context of citizenship. First, they were concerned that they might become unwilling agents of the Home Office, part of the process of deciding who could or could not become a British citizen. Second, they felt under pressure to become experts in a new range of additional subjects – parliament, the law, the electoral system, UK geography and history. Third, there was confusion. Were they teachers of ESOL or teachers of citizenship?

The ESOL teachers thought the learners would not find the areas like citizenship, parliament and the electoral system interesting. In fact, through questionnaires and focus groups, learners reported they had enjoyed these aspects of the course most. Perhaps this was because the topics felt more adult, more abstract or perhaps because they were fed up of talking about 'Going to the doctor'.

Some ESOL learners have a sophisticated understanding of citizenship, they simply do not have the English language to express the complexity of the concept. For this reason, it is important to draw on the experience of the learners and devise strategies to help them to express their understanding in English. As adults, they will all have experience of living in at least two different countries and will be able to comment on the similarities and differences of being citizens in their country of origin and in the UK.

Refugees are often in exile because of their political activity in their own country. In this way, they may have been very active citizens. Some refugees bear the physical and mental scars of the consequences of their activities, tortured by oppressive regimes.

This makes citizenship a very pertinent topic for the ESOL classroom but also a potentially complex and painful one. The learners may not wish to share their experience of political struggle, conflict and exile. Others may welcome the opportunity to talk about their beliefs and passions. I taught one group of Kurdish refugees in Tower Hamlets in the 1990s. We were learning expression of likes and dislikes – 'I like tea, I like coffee, I don't like tea…'. One learner broke free, he'd had enough small talk – 'I like democracy, I like freedom'. That taught me.

I met the same group on a demonstration some months later. There were more opportunities for speaking and listening at Entry 1 level there than I had ever managed to create in the classroom. There were lots of language practice opportunities in that noisy, vibrant crowd with shouted slogans, angry exchanges and speeches to the crowd.

If you work in adult education, discussions on citizenship issues often arise informally. During the trialling of the learning materials, a consultant reported on his visit to one of the pilot sites. The Appeal Court decision that a Muslim schoolgirl had been unlawfully excluded from her Luton school for wearing traditional Muslim dress had just been announced.

> *My final visit coincided with another national event; Shabina Begum's jilbab court case. With a group of Entry 3 level learners, mostly young mothers and their children, I sat round a table piled high with doughnuts, cakes and fruit for the end-of-pilot learner focus group. After a rather formalised discussion to get my 'data', the Shabina Begum case came up, and all hell broke loose. The Iraqi woman was in favour of the court's decision – so was the Sudanese. The woman from the Ivory Coast was dead against, and so was her friend from Niger. The Ethiopian was in favour – the Iranian woman seemed more occupied with the doughnuts. Several small and jammy children ran crazily around the room, high on sugar. The argument raged back and forth, passionately. Eventually one of them asked me what I thought.*

> *'This' I said, overcome with emotion, 'is exactly what a citizenship class should be like.*

> *They looked at me as if I was a crazy man.*
>   (John Sutter, LLU+, report on ESOL citizenship pilot project, March 2005)

Learners involved in the pilot process had lots to say about citizenship:

> *I like to know places and traditions about G.B. It really made me think about our society.*
>
> (Thomas Danby College learner)

> *We liked the team work. We learned about UK culture, everybody brings different ideas, we all mix, different religions and cultures.*
>
> (Apex training centre, Leicester learner)

The opportunity to learn ESOL in the context of citizenship is the opportunity to make explicit the multicultural aspects of British life, which this learner valued so much. It is not about learning how to be a citizen because ESOL learners are adults who are already citizens of their own country. Neither is it about learning to be like the British, whatever that may be. It is rather about being a citizen in Britain, an individual within a community within a nation. The learners and teachers who worked with NIACE in the pilot of the learning materials realised this opportunity. The process of developing the *Citizenship Materials for ESOL Learners* is described in the next chapter.

Chapter 4

The ESOL citizenship project

Introduction

Citizenship Materials for ESOL Learners was a development project led by NIACE and LLU+ as part of the government's strategy to make becoming a UK citizen a more meaningful event. From November 2005, the two routes to naturalisation were in place. Applicants with sufficient English language skills could take an online, multiple-choice citizenship test, *Life in the UK*, at any of the 100 Life in the UK Test Centres. Applicants who needed to improve their English language skills could follow an ESOL course using the new *Citizenship Materials for ESOL Learners* pack.

The project started in February 2004 with the development of a suggested syllabus for ESOL citizenship. Then a draft pack of learning

Delegates at one of the familiarisation workshops

materials was developed and trialled with 18 ESOL providers. The pilots were selected to trial the pack with different target groups – refugees, settled immigrants and new arrivals. A national teacher-training programme was set up, delivering one-day workshops for ESOL teachers. The pack was then revised, taking into account the recommendations of the teachers who piloted the materials and the delegates who attended the first phase of teachers' workshops.

The website www.esolcitizenship.org.uk went live in September 2005, and provides each section of the pack in a PDF format and also as a Word document so that teachers can download and adapt the learning materials.

Prior to the launch of the Scottish pack, there was some debate on the Home Office language requirements for citizenship and the equivalent requirements for England or Scotland. The Home Office requires applicants for citizenship to achieve 'two SQA units at Access level'. The issue is now resolved and applicants whose English is considered to be *below Intermediate 1 (Entry 3)* must take an ESOL

A trainer at the Northern Ireland workshops

qualification, at the appropriate level for them, in speaking and listening. In Scotland, this is two ESOL Units at Access Level under the Scottish Credit and Qualifications Framework approved by the Scottish Qualification Authority. As in the rest of the UK, applicants should have studied for this qualification in an ESOL class using a citizenship context.

In 2006, NIACE and LLU+ recruited writers to adapt the pack for ESOL learners in Northern Ireland, under the guidance of an Advisory Group. The writers were themselves ESOL practitioners from Northern Ireland.

Issues

Language focus

The teacher's task is to teach ESOL in the context of citizenship but this is not always easy. During the piloting of the materials, consultants visited the ESOL providers and observed lessons in progress. They noted that some teachers, distracted by teaching citizenship, seemed to have lost the language learning focus. The 'information' of citizenship was delivered effectively but the language points were lost in the unloading of content. In the revised pack, language points were added to the teachers' notes, giving clear instructions on the points to be taught, including differentiation, extension activities and additional materials.

Speaking, listening and levels

There is a significant difference in the demands of the two routes to satisfy the language requirements for citizenship. By taking the *Life in the UK* test, a citizenship applicant demonstrates that they have reading skills above Entry Level 3. Although language is not specifically tested, by successfully passing the online test, applicants show they have reading and comprehension skills at this level.

However, if an applicant follows an ESOL citizenship course, the individual must, as a minimum, gain an ESOL *Skills for Life* qualification in speaking and listening. This means that in England, Wales and Northern Ireland the ESOL learner is not required to demonstrate reading skills to satisfy the language requirements for citizenship. In Scotland, however, the ESOL learner who wants to apply for citizenship only needs to complete two Units at Access Level (a level lower than Entry Level 1). Access 2 comprises all four language skills (speaking, listening, reading and writing) and the class teacher is the assessor. ESOL *Skills for Life* qualifications, on the other hand, are externally assessed. From a practical point of view, the Scottish Qualifications Authority qualifications reflect the citizenship syllabus. For example, at Access 3, Transactional English includes tasks such as reading a train timetable, registering with a doctor (speaking), writing a note to a teacher explaining the absence of a child and changing an appointment with a doctor (listening).

It could be argued that this is a contradiction between the language requirements for the Citizenship Test applicant and those for the ESOL citizenship course applicant, which favours the individual with a lower English language level. On the other hand, one might argue that this is an open and inclusive procedure which acknowledges and accommodates difference. Not everyone can speak a foreign language with the same degree of competence. The significance is that an applicant has demonstrated a willingness to engage with the UK community by learning the language, at whatever level.

Teachers or writers

The consultants observed some outstanding practice during the pilot of the learning materials. The teachers delivered imaginative and exciting sessions combining learning activities from the pack and materials they had written themselves. However, some teachers were reluctant to share the learning materials they had written or adapted from the draft pack. When they did submit learning materials, the accompanying teachers' guidance notes were sometimes unclear. A team of ESOL staff at LLU+ edited the materials to bring a consistent approach and to write explicit detailed instructions for the teachers' use. The best

Delegates at the familiarisation workshop in Cookstown, Northern Ireland

teachers, it seemed, were not always the best writers of materials but a team approach, combining teachers' and writers' skills, achieved the desired result.

Feedback from teachers and learners

Teachers reported that the citizenship materials pack had introduced subject matter which was of interest to learners and it had been particularly successful with more controversial and less functional topics, like Human Rights. All the sections worked well. A consultant reported:

> *I've observed some lessons where the materials have generated considerable interest and discussion. This has been true especially on those sections that deal with issues less frequently covered in ESOL lessons – Section 2 on Parliament and Section 6 on Human Rights.*

Outside speakers were invited into the classrooms, to give learners direct contact with relevant organisations and agencies, emphasise authenticity and give learners increased information on, and understanding of, citizenship issues. They were generally very popular. However, teachers felt that the guest speakers needed to be language-aware and able to communicate effectively at the appropriate level.

Outside speakers were popular with learners. The majority said they would welcome more visitors and speakers to the class and would enjoy more visits to historical sites. When asked in focus groups who they would like to invite, learners suggested a local MP, local councillor, representatives from local services like hospitals, police or education providers, a union representative, a local charity, a DfES minister, David Beckham and Tony Blair!

In one focus group, a learner said the materials pack helped them to feel more connected with British society.

> *It has been very useful and helpful and I would recommend it to other students.*

> (Tower Hamlets College learner)

Who knows more?

There is an interesting paradox which may grow as the citizenship tests and courses become well established. The new citizens who successfully pass the test or complete an ESOL citizenship course may well know more about the UK than their UK-born neighbours. Even when citizenship has been part of the school curriculum for some years, the poor quality of provision, as highlighted by the Chief Inspector, may mean that individuals schooled in the UK never catch up with new migrants. Does this matter? It is interesting to note how many of the newspapers covering the launch of the Citizenship Test in November 2005 remarked that most people could not pass the test.

Perhaps the individual in the street would not know the functions of the two Houses of Parliament, the numbers to dial for emergencies or the most likely places in England to see thatched cottages.

As good as the teacher

The materials pack, *Citizenship Materials for ESOL Learners*, is only as good as the teacher who delivers it. Like most learning resources, the materials need adapting to meet the needs of each group of learners. This takes time and resources. It also needs a skilled teacher to use the content to teach the language points rather than simply convey information about, for example, the local library, registering with a GP or the workings of Parliament. The materials, like all ESOL materials, need to be adapted for learners.

Going local

It is important that the ESOL and citizenship course is firmly located in the local. The new citizen needs to see their role in the local community and the possibility of influencing the community through local politics. The *Citizenship Materials for ESOL Learners* pack gives examples of learning activities but local resources will have to be collected by the teacher. It is probable that the ESOL teacher will find that some learners in any group are already active citizens – helping out in their child's school, interpreting for friends or running supplementary schools. It is essential these skills are recognised and the learners' experiences valued.

The teachers' views

Some teachers from Croydon took part in trialling the learning materials and one wrote about her experience:

TRIALLING CITIZENSHIP MATERIALS

In the run-up to the introduction of the Citizenship Test for people applying for British citizenship, we at Croydon CETS have been privileged to share in trialling appropriate ESOL materials…. Our three groups of learners opted predictably to study health and education but also chose less frequently covered subjects like 'human rights', 'community involvement', 'Britain as a diverse society', 'Parliament and the electoral system' and 'law'. We had to work harder than we expected adapting and preparing materials before trialling them.

In some cases we had difficulty 'selling' the citizenship concept to our learners. However, when we described it as 'things you need to know about living in the UK' we got a more positive response. Another problem was that at the lower level we found it hard in such an information-heavy course to provide the structured speaking practice that learners need and it was not always easy to find/create appropriate listening materials. The real value of the exercise for us lay in extending our repertoire as teachers. It was good to be obliged to get information about aspects of British life we were hazy about, to get our classes searching on the Internet and to organise visits and guest speakers. Our learners, on the whole, responded with enthusiasm. They particularly enjoyed a visit to the Mayor's parlour – 'We loved seeing your robes, your insignia, your big chair, your big office. Please invite us again!'.

Joanna Lane, Croydon CETS

Learners in Croydon on a visit to the Mayor's parlour (Croydon CETS)

Another teacher from the pilots wrote of her experience of trialling the materials:

MY EXPERIENCE OF TEACHING THE CITIZENSHIP COURSE

I have been teaching citizenship with students since January. I have enjoyed the teaching very much and some of the students have enjoyed it enormously and found it very interesting, whilst some others have said they aren't interested in politics and others said would like to do more grammar. Because of the time constraints of wanting to use as much of the materials as I could before the trials finished, I didn't do as much grammar as usual. Ten weeks is obviously not enough time in which to cover this course when you only see students once or twice a week. I feel two terms is more realistic and would make it possible to do more grammar work as one went along. For example, the Suffragette lesson highlighted how poor my students were at question forms, so the next lesson we focused on that for the first hour.

... A considerable amount of knowledge or time spent doing research is required in order to do justice to this course and also to be able to answer all the questions students might put to you. I never seemed to have enough of that.

There are so many events happening all the time in the news which are wonderful resources for the course. For example, I had arranged a visit by our local MP for today, but he was unable to come due to the all-night sitting in the House for Tony Blair's Anti-Terrorist Bill. I ended up buying the newspapers on the way to college in case this happened, and used an article on this for reading comprehension, summary writing and extending their understanding of the way our laws, Parliament and the House of Lords work.

... I organised a day trip to London for all the classes trialling the materials and that was a great focus for a lot of the teaching too. Good fun was had by all! So – the materials? A great new teaching resource (to be built on) for ESOL in my opinion.

Wendy J Morgan

Chapter 5
Learning activities

Introduction

In the last chapter, we saw that the pilot of *Citizenship Materials for ESOL Learners* threw up a number of interesting issues. They also produced some stimulating ideas for learning activities. Some were built up and included in the pack and some others are described in this chapter. The ESOL teachers who participated in the trial of the materials found citizenship a challenging context in which to teach language, as Wendy Morgan described in the previous chapter. Some of their ideas to meet the challenge are described here.

These activities, as stressed in previous chapters, should be adapted for a number of reasons. First, all ESOL learning materials should be made relevant and useful to the learners and adapted for their skills levels and personal interests. Second, the activities, if possible, should be linked to local events, politics, people or communities. Third, the materials may date. Some, like the learning activities in the pack on the Cabinet or the minimum wage, will be out of date in a few years and so it is the ESOL teacher's responsibility to update them.

If possible, the learning activity should be used in 'real time' so that the group learns about Eid at the end of Ramadan, Guy Fawkes in November or voting when there is a general or local election.

There is already a wide range of excellent ESOL resources published on health, housing, education and employment, so they are not covered here. This chapter describes instead some ideas on how to teach:

- What is citizenship?
- Parliament and the electoral system
- Geography and history of the UK
- Diversity in the UK

- Community engagement
- Human rights

Some additional sources of information are also recommended in this chapter but should be treated with caution. For example, the website Wikipedia is an excellent online resource but the teacher should expect occasional inaccuracies. Wikipedia is also available in other languages, including Spanish, Portuguese and Polish, so it may be a useful resource for learners, too. The Spartacus website is a British online encyclopaedia with excellent articles on historical topics but it is designed for school students and would need to be adapted. It is a free resource with lots of useful images.

What is citizenship?

Although this is a challenging topic to cover, especially with Entry Level 1 learners, many of the teachers and learners on the pilot project found this the most interesting. It is a discussion you may decide to have at the end of a course, rather than the beginning, when learners have developed some of the vocabulary for the discussion of abstract concepts. Teachers from Brighton, Hove and Sussex Sixth Form College started with the question, 'What makes you feel part of the UK?' They asked learners to interview each other and then write a short piece on what they thought was most essential for integration. Using learners' writing as a stimulus for discussion or further writing usually works well. These learners gave their reasons for choosing 'understanding the English language' as the answer to the question.

Language is the only way for people to communicate with each other. When you live in a country, you become a citizen so you must learn the language because it helps you to communicate everywhere you go, for example in offices or banks, travelling in the city, your shopping. … You can say what you think, give your opinions, join in a meeting to discuss and plan action, read newspapers about the government and the community where you live.

*It seems to me you have to build your personality from scratch
again to manage in a foreign language. I'm trying to develop my
speaking and listening skills to improve my understanding of
others and learn how to explain my thoughts in the right way –
anger, love and lots of other emotions. Of course, making
friends at the moment can be a problem because of the
language barriers.*

(Learners from Brighton, Hove and Sussex Sixth Form College)

Parliament and the electoral system

Another idea from Brighton, Hove and Sussex Sixth Form College used
Economic Citizenship, materials designed for schools, and developed
this into an extension exercise on government spending. Learners
worked in groups as political parties and discussed: how much the
government spent each year, what this was spent on, who paid for it
and how money was raised. Groups were given money to spend and
roles to play – the Chancellor, ministers responsible for transport, law
and order, health, education, and so on. The learners then discussed in
groups how they would spend the national budget and why.

This would be an ideal learning activity to conduct at the time of a
general election when lots of real material would be available for
stimulating discussion. This could be developed into a role-play or
preparation for a visiting speaker such as a local councillor or MP.

At the higher levels, learners could compare the tax systems in the
countries they know and discuss direct tax and indirect tax in the UK.

Teachers at Croydon CETS developed a whole learning activity
including a role-play using one picture of an abandoned car from a
local authority website.

The enlarged picture was displayed on the board and learners were asked, 'What's wrong with this car?' The teacher elicited vocabulary about the damaged car (broken windscreen, flat tyre) and then asked learners if they would worry if the car were parked outside for three weeks. They moved on to an exercise which was a series of statements about the car:

I'd like to report...

It has been here for...

It's an old...

The windscreen is...

Finally, learners worked in pairs to practise and then perform a role-play between a caller and council officer.

This type of approach can be used with any local issue as stimulus; for example, a pedestrian crossing needed at the local school. Learners can work in groups to write to the local MP, design a flyer, organise a petition, find out the local councillor's surgery times, research local statistics and write to the local newspaper.

UK geography and history

Geography is a great context in which to teach English language with lots of opportunities for prepositions! More importantly, learners who trialled the materials enjoyed the geography and history far more than was expected. As ever, it is important to start with the learners' knowledge and work from there. Some learners may come from a Commonwealth country where British and European history has been comprehensively, and perhaps disproportionately, taught. Others may need to compare their own country to the UK. A learner in Hackney once told me she came from Somalia, which she described as 'a small country in Africa'. She was very surprised when she was told that Britain was less than half the size of Somalia. It is all relative. A teacher from London told me another anecdote which illustrates this well. A

Learners from the Chinese Centre (North of England) study a map

group of learners, Kurdish refugees who had lived in Hackney, East London for some years, was offered a lift to Heathrow airport in West London. As they drove through the West End they admired the Oxford Street lights saying, 'This is beautiful. Where are we? This is nothing like London.' Their life in exile in Britain had centred around their community in Hackney and they had not travelled anywhere else. It is unsurprising that asylum seekers who may have been dispersed in the UK under the National Asylum Support Service (NASS), and may have been moved several times, are disoriented and do not have a clear understanding of the relative geography of their new home.

Starting where the learner is, the following activity could be used as a stimulus for learning about the symbols of the UK or the geography and history of the four countries of the UK. Teachers at the Chinese Centre (North of England) devised a very successful learning activity using the pound coins in the learners' pockets. Learners were asked to look at all the coins and find as many variations as possible. The Welsh leek, Celtic Cross, English Oak and Scottish thistle represented on the

coins were discussed and the teacher explained what the symbols were and which countries they were associated with. This also presented an opportunity to tell learners of the two official languages in Wales as the inscription on one of the designs reads: '*PLEIDIOL, WYF I'M GWLAD*' ('True am I to my country').

Another activity from the same centre looked at flags. The teacher gave out the flags, asked learners if they recognised them and what they represented. Using a map of the UK, the learners were asked to point out the four countries and to match the flags to the countries. The construction of the Union Jack was explained as were the differences between the terms 'United Kingdom', 'England' and 'Britain'. Using the visual images promoted a discussion and, as an extension exercise, the learners went to on discuss patron Saints and Saint days. Saint days would offer an opportunity for a consolidation exercise in 'real time' when the day was celebrated. For example, learners would revise what they learned about St Patrick on St Patrick's Day, 17 March.

Learners at the Chinese Centre (North of England) in a session on flags

The sessions involved a lot of oral work through class discussion, a lucky dip knowledge exercise, jigsaw exercise, questions and answers, discussion of images and a knowledge test at the end.

The geography and history was popular with learners if it involved visiting speakers or going out on trips to places of interest. In the feedback, teachers from the pilots stressed it was important to use local resources. These included the National Glass Centre in Sunderland, the Jewry Wall in Leicester and Alnwick Castle in Northumberland. Teachers brought in leaflets, information on admission times, prices and photographs or asked learners at Entry Level 3 to research this on the Internet. For learners working towards Entry Level 1, simplified forms were developed using the information from the leaflets. Learners were asked to make phone enquiries or use a fax to obtain further information. Most teachers said they developed quizzes to complete during the trip along with follow-up activities for use afterwards. For example, learners made a brochure for other learners about the place of interest or wrote postcards. However, teachers pointed out that it was also important to 'Have fun!'

The UK as a diverse society

As with the other topics, while the possibilities are endless, the focus needs to be maintained on language learning. The learning resources to support the topics of diversity in society, cross-cultural issues, body language and festivals are considerable and we will look at a small selection of them here. The learners themselves are a key resource and their experience and reflections on contemporary British society can be used as texts for comprehension or as presentations. It is also important to give a historical context and to mention, for example, the presence of black people in Britain under the Romans and the long history of gypsies and travellers in the UK.

Teachers from Hull suggested a focus on body language: burping, yawning, queuing, shaking hands, giving up your seat on the bus and standing on the right side of the escalator. With this focus, learners could have a discussion on what is acceptable in their culture and in the UK, and perhaps use role-play to explore different situations. Teachers from Sheffield College used the website from Woodlands School which has a 'Do's and Don'ts' page, including:

- *Do stand in line*
- *Do say 'Excuse me'*
- *Do pay as you go*
- *Do say 'Please' and 'Thank you'*
- *Do not greet people with a kiss*
- *Do not talk loudly in public*
- *Do not stare at anyone in public*

The learners would have plenty to discuss from this list as norms are culture-specific and also may apply in the countryside but not in some UK cities. Learners from Open Doors in Bournemouth completed a very interesting extension exercise from this list and wrote similar guides to their own countries. The results could be used for a 'compare and contrast' activity and as a discussion stimulus for ESOL learners in other groups. One learner wrote a guide to her birthplace, the Democratic Republic of Congo:

- *Use the local currency and not foreign currency because they will think you are rich and charge you more money.*
- *Don't ask for a doggy bag in a restaurant. It is rude.*
- *Have some money in your pocket for bribes everywhere.*
- *Don't take photographs in public places.*
- *If someone invites you to a party, or out somewhere, you don't pay anything.*
- *Never be on time if you have an invitation: if you are, it means you are there to help. If you are late, you are there just as a guest.*
- *It's impolite to leave food on your plate in a home. It means the food is not good.*
- *If you are offered food, it's very rude to refuse. You must at least taste it.*

Similar comparisons of what is acceptable in one culture but not in another can be made using the television as a resource. The HSBC bank ran a series of advertisements recently based on body language and different meanings of gestures across the world. They might amuse learners and would be easily understood at Entry Level 1 to convey the complexities of culture-specific behaviour.

The topic of body language might be particularly important for ESOL learners in custodial settings. With limited English language skills, learners working towards Entry Level 1 who are prisoners may find that effective non-verbal communication is a principal resource. In a stressful and volatile environment, misunderstanding of another's body language could lead to conflict or violence. As prisoners have no access to the Internet and limited access to external resources, the ESOL teacher would have to develop photos and flashcards to practise speaking and listening skills within the context of appropriate body language. Questions around emotions, such as 'How do you feel?' might be used to expand vocabulary and also develop cross-cultural awareness.

Teachers from Newcastle suggested using different festivals which related to the learners' cultures and to the local area. They gave as examples Chinese New Year and the Turkish festival, Şeker Bayram. They used extracts from local newspapers, adapted them and developed a grid. The learners interviewed each other about a particular festival and used the grid as a writing frame to describe the festival fully. This could then be used to consolidate writing, practise paragraphing and linking words and phrases. At lower levels, teachers asked learners to scan the texts for dates and enter them on a class calendar. This work could also be used to practise prepositions of time: Bonfire night is *in* November, Bonfire night is *on* the 5th of November.

Teachers at an event in Bristol suggested including other national events such as Comic Relief and Pancake Day. The festivals should be taught in 'real time' and be those which would be interesting for the group. At Entry Levels 1 and 2 the teachers suggested listening and speaking activities with artefacts and visual aids as prompts. At Entry Level 3, learners could do research on the Internet and as an extension exercise perhaps discuss the commercialism of festivals. One of the best-known multicultural resources for this work is the SHAP calendar of religious festivals (see Resources, p. 69).

An EFL teacher in Brazil posted this example of cross-cultural misunderstanding on the British Council website:

Others are baffled by the way the British speak English

This is what the speaker really means:

What they say:	What is understood:	What they mean:
I'm sure it's my fault	It is his fault	It is your fault
I'll bear it in mind	He'll probably do it	I will do nothing about it
Correct me if I'm wrong	Tell me what you think	I know I'm right – please don't contradict me
With the greatest respect	He is listening to me	I think you are wrong or a fool

(From a message posted to the British Council, Brazil ELT online community; www.britishcouncil.org.br/elt)

Community engagement – volunteering

The idea of mentors for new citizens was one that was promoted by Sir Bernard Crick and the Life in the United Kingdom Advisory Group. The group recommended that a register be set up of local people who were willing to mentor and befriend new citizens.

However, mentoring can be as valuable if the roles are reversed. To be eligible to apply for UK citizenship, ESOL learners must have already lived in the UK for at least five years. As well as *being* mentored, those individuals can *be* mentors or volunteers or become involved in their local community in a whole range of ways. They have experience of living and working in the UK, they may have children in schools and they will have used the local services, medical care and support agencies.

The teachers involved in the pilots identified several interesting learning activities around volunteering. They found that learners were already active in their own community organisations: for example, Somali learners were organising an after-school group for children. Other learners were involved in mother-and-toddler groups and playgroups. Simply asking a group of ESOL learners what community activities they are already involved in will provide a resource for learning and teaching. They may interpret for friends and neighbours, assist at the local mosque, teach at supplementary schools or support youth groups. Learners may be willing to do a presentation on their experiences.

Some teachers invited guest speakers from the Citizens Advice Bureau, Refugee Action and other local agencies to talk to the group. However, they advised that speakers needed to briefed fully so that the language of the presentation was at the appropriate level. Some speakers found it too difficult to simplify their language. One group had a foster carer as a speaker. Learners in another group chose a local charity, researched the organisation, then raised money for the charity by planning an event and bringing in food to sell in the centre. This involved research skills, note-making, report-writing and an oral presentation.

Other learners were encouraged to go to the local volunteer bureau, charity shops, schools and local library to enquire about opportunities for volunteering. This involved making requests, listening for information and understanding a text.

Apart from the intrinsic value of volunteering, there is an extrinsic value for learners without previous work experience in the UK. Refugees who have fled their country of origin without papers proving their qualifications and work experience often find it extremely difficult to find work. The opportunity to volunteer and gain work experience and a reference from a UK employer is invaluable.

Human rights

ESOL teachers are already aware of the experiences of some learners, especially asylum-seekers and refugees, who have suffered mental and physical abuse. All aspects of human rights need to be treated sensitively in the classroom and some topics may not be appropriate for particular individuals; they may be too sensitive and painful. However, the evidence from piloting the citizenship materials showed that most learners enjoyed this area of work and found it perhaps more challenging and engaging than most usual practical topics of everyday English.

At Croydon Continuing Education and Training Service (CETS), teachers developed two sessions that worked particularly well. The sessions had three aims, to enable learners to:

- discuss human rights issues;
- obtain information from detailed reading; and
- make a short presentation.

The teacher elicited from learners what they knew about International Women's Day, and they compared different countries and how they mark the day. Learners read a text, either as a class or in pairs, then completed a timeline, adding information from their own countries. The teacher then elicited the names of women who had made a difference to the lives of others. In small groups, learners were given a different profile of a famous woman and asked to complete information below a photo. The groups then swapped information to complete data on all the women.

For a second session on inequality, the teacher prepared six short texts on women and work, health, education, homelessness, violence, and business and government. Learners were invited to discuss whether or not they think inequalities exist and why. Then they were told they were going to make short presentations in groups. The teacher revised the format of presentations – a greeting, the title, giving the presentation using appropriate clarity and phrases, speed of delivery, giving thanks, and taking questions. Each group prepared a presentation from a different text, using their own words. As each group made their presentation, the other learners completed a question-and-answer sheet on all six topics.

In this chapter, we looked at a number of stimulating ideas for learning activities using citizenship as a context in which to teach language. These activities should be adapted and be made relevant and useful to the learners and also be linked to local events and communities. In the next chapter, models of provision are described and some case studies are given as examples.

Chapter 6
ESOL and citizenship provision

Introduction

In this chapter we will look at different models of ESOL and citizenship provision, some implications, the ESOL qualifications and the evidence required by the Home Office for citizenship application. There is also a checklist of questions to direct the ESOL teacher to the most relevant topics for individual learners.

If you are an ESOL manager or teacher planning provision, there is a number of models you may wish to consider.

Model 1:	Citizenship integrated in all Entry Level ESOL provision
Model 2:	ESOL and citizenship courses as separate provision
Model 3:	ESOL and citizenship module
Model 4:	Citizenship courses – prepare for the test

Model 1: Citizenship integrated in all provision

You may choose to integrate some citizenship content into all your Entry Level ESOL courses. This would entail using materials from the *Citizenship Materials for ESOL Learners* pack for at least 20 hours of the course delivery. This is easily done as most Entry Level courses would include some language work on health, housing, work or education. All of these are topics in the pack. You do not have to use the learning activities as published and, in fact, you are encouraged to adapt the materials.

As a provider, you will probably want to keep records to show that each course has included the citizenship element. It is quite likely that these ESOL courses will comprise both learners applying for naturalisation and those who are not and the citizenship materials can be used regardless, as an integral part of the course.

The advantage of this model is that you do not need to signpost learners at initial assessment depending on whether they do or do not intend to apply for citizenship. Rather, any learner can be given a pro forma letter at the end of the course (see References, p. XX).

A disadvantage might be the implications of differentiation. With mixed levels of learners in the class with different learning goals, there might be an increased workload for the teacher in differentiating materials. This seems to be the most common type of provision at present. In a small sample of 31 ESOL providers, 21 offered citizenship for naturalisation embedded in all their ESOL courses.

Model 2: ESOL and citizenship as separate provision

You may opt for separate provision, which is advertised as ESOL for citizenship in the prospectus and recruits only learners who wish to apply for naturalisation. This may attract learners who are looking for a course to lead to citizenship. It may also make it easier for other agencies to signpost learners to your provision. One of the advantages of this type of course is that there is likely to be a more homogeneous group of learners. Another is that the teachers can specialise in this course and build up a bank of learning materials. This model was offered by 13 of the 31 ESOL providers we contacted.

Model 3: ESOL and citizenship module

Another model chosen by some providers is a 'bolt-on' 20-hour module to fast-track learners through the citizenship requirements as an addition to the ESOL *Skills for Life* course they are following. The advantage of this model is that learners may not have citizenship as a specific goal when they enrol at the college but while following their course they become aware of the options. The model is likely to be sustainable as you can draw learners from other courses.

Model 4: Prepare for the test

Since the introduction of the *Life in the UK* test in November 2005, entrepreneurs have seized the opportunity to provide 'Prepare for the Test' short courses for individuals who plan to take the citizenship test. Some very different courses have emerged, provided by private businesses, training agencies, community organisations, local authorities and colleges.

These courses are, by default, only really suitable for individuals with English language reading skills above Entry Level 3 and some confidence in using IT. Some imaginative short courses have been developed in libraries, museums and colleges to maximise the learners' chances of passing the test by studying the Home Office handbook *Life in the United Kingdom: A Journey to Citizenship* and testing learners' recall of the information in the book.

For example, Norwich Castle hosted a course in the museum over five weeks. Learners handled the artefacts in the museum to bring the history to life and learned the key chapters together. At Leicester College, learners attended a 20-hour course and discussed the information together. Since there is no LSC funding for such courses, providers must seek alternative sources of funding or charge the learners a fee.

There are some disadvantages to this model. One is that some agencies have set up courses and charged individuals very high fees for courses of dubious quality. The learners may be under the misapprehension that a course is necessary whereas the only essential is learning the information in the Home Office handbook. Learners may pay a fee for the course, then the £34 test fee and fail repeatedly. In fact, UfI reports that some individuals have failed the test up to ten times, the most common cause of test failure being lack of English language and comprehension skills. Some agencies have recruited learners at language levels below Entry Level 3 who have very little chance of passing the test.

Because the test only takes 45 minutes and costs £34, some applicants for citizenship may be persuaded to sit the test rather than take the time to complete a one-year ESOL course. In this case, the learning adviser has a crucial role to play in giving the applicant informed advice based on an initial assessment of ESOL skills.

Implications and issues

Each of the models has implications for delivery. Walsall and Sheffield Colleges both took part in the pilot and the teachers reflected on some of the implications. The teachers' knowledge of the topics and their confidence in delivery was a concern, especially in the topics which are less common in the ESOL syllabus. The teachers needed increased preparation time for the newer topics, like Parliament or human rights, and for differentiation of materials. They also thought that the information would need updating frequently. Health, housing and work were perceived as easy topics to integrate into the usual ESOL syllabus.

The language difficulties faced by learners at Entry Level 1 when hosting a guest speaker was another issue. Teachers reported that some speakers could not simplify their language to make it more accessible for Entry Level learners.

However, the overwhelming feedback from learners was positive about the learning activities and the topics they chose. Some learners from Sheffield College and Walsall College commented:

"I enjoyed the topics and found them easy to read."

"I found the information useful in settling in to the community."

"The information about the political system was beneficial and interesting."

"I was really happy to learn about concepts of citizenship and the words used, for example, morals. This has helped me to understand."

"I would have liked to do more on values, beliefs and the culture of England."

"*I particularly enjoyed learning about Parliament and finding information about MPs on the internet.*"

"*Using the case studies and role play was fun.*"

Teachers from Sheffield and Walsall made the following recommendations for ESOL citizenship teachers:

- Bring in relevant articles and information.
- Share the workload by regularly scanning Internet sites for updates.
- Produce an ESOL citizenship resource bank.
- Produce a website list.
- Make ESOL citizenship a fixed item in team meetings to drive the momentum.

Accreditation and evidence for inspection

In all cases, to apply for citizenship, learners need to obtain an ESOL *Skills for Life* qualification at any Entry Level. The ESOL qualifications for citizenship are exactly the same as those for all other ESOL learners. The certificates do not refer to ESOL with citizenship because there is no citizenship curriculum. Awarding bodies do not know which candidates use the certificates for naturalisation purposes. The citizenship element is based on teachers delivering ESOL courses using *Citizenship Materials for ESOL Learners* as an appropriate part of individual learning plans. Quality assurance of this is through the normal Adult Learning Inspectorate (ALI)/Ofsted inspection processes.

Learners who wish to apply for citizenship have to supply a copy of the awarding body's *Skills for Life* ESOL certificate to the Home Office with their application. Together with a pro forma letter from the college confirming that this certificate was gained from a course that delivered ESOL in a citizenship context, this will meet the language requirements. The pro forma for the letter has been developed by the Learning and Skills Council and is available on the LSC website as Factsheet 7 (see References, p. 69).

Applicants must achieve the ESOL qualification in at least speaking and listening. In England, this is a *Skills for Life* ESOL qualification in speaking and listening at Entry Levels 1, 2 or 3. In Scotland, this is two ESOL units at Access Level under the Scottish Credit and Qualifications Framework, approved by the Scottish Qualification Authority (SQA). From a practical point of view, the SQA qualifications sit very well with the citizenship syllabus. At Access Level 3, the Transactional English has, as an outcome, tasks such as reading a train timetable, registering with a doctor, writing a note to a teacher explaining the absence of a child, and changing an appointment with a doctor.

There is no fixed time limit for achieving the ESOL qualification so learners can take as long as they need. The ESOL course needs to be long enough for the individual to achieve the qualification, which can be 'banked' so that they can apply for citizenship later.

A checklist to choose the topics

As an ESOL teacher or manager, you will select the citizenship topics most relevant for the learners you work with. You will not have time to

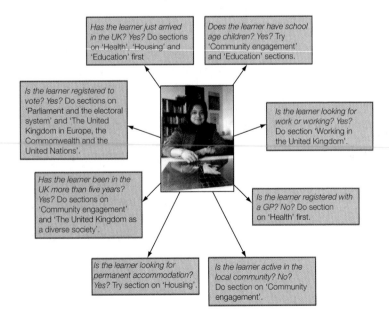

Has the learner just arrived in the UK? Yes? Do sections on 'Health', 'Housing' and 'Education' first

Does the learner have school age children? Yes? Try 'Community engagement' and 'Education' sections.

Is the learner registered to vote? Yes? Do sections on 'Parliament and the electoral system' and 'The United Kingdom in Europe, the Commonwealth and the United Nations'.

Is the learner looking for work or working? Yes? Do section 'Working in the United Kingdom'.

Has the learner been in the UK more than five years? Yes? Do sections on 'Community engagement' and 'The United Kingdom as a diverse society'.

Is the learner registered with a GP? No? Do section on 'Health' first.

Is the learner looking for permanent accommodation? Yes? Try section on 'Housing'.

Is the learner active in the local community? No? Do section on 'Community engagement'.

cover all the topics suggested and not all of them will be relevant for your learners. This checklist of questions may help you choose the most relevant topics, assuming that you are working with a mixed group of learners, some of whom wish to apply for citizenship and some of whom do not.

Parliament and the electoral system

- *How long has the learner been in the UK?*
  If they have just arrived, this topic is not the priority. If they have been here for some years, they may be interested in the system of government. If the learner has studied to a higher level abroad, they may have already studied civics, citizenship or parliamentary systems. As always, ask the learner.

Geography and history of the United Kingdom

- *Where is the learner living?*
  Start local. The learner needs to know about the local area, the region and the country – Scotland, Wales, Northern Ireland or England.

- *Does the learner have some knowledge of the geography of the local area in which s/he is living?*
  Prioritise this if the learner is a new arrival in the area, particularly if they have been dispersed. This can be disorienting and the learner needs to locate themselves in the country.

- *Does the learner have some knowledge of the history of the local area in which s/he is living?*
  The learner who has been here longer may find local history and the way it has shaped the local town and economy interesting. The learner may already have learnt some British history at school – check first. Some learners may choose to do this section for fun.

The UK as a diverse society

- *Where are you teaching?*
  If you work in an area without a minority ethnic community, the demographic profile of the UK may not be obvious. It is important to help the learner get the broader picture.

- *Is it a multicultural area?*
  If you are teaching in an inner city it may be very evident that Britain is a diverse society. Use the local statistics on ethnicity as a learning resource. Using national statistics is helpful as a basis for comparison too, so that the learner learns about all the different communities in the UK.

- *Is the learner in a mixed class with lots of nationalities represented?*
  The learners themselves may be the best resource for learning about different religions and cultures first-hand.

Human rights

- *Is the learner an asylum-seeker or refugee?*
  Treat this section with care and, as always, treat the learner with respect. Whilst some asylum-seekers and refugees are willing to talk about their experience of forced exile and find it helpful, for others it may be too painful. Be guided by the learner. It is still useful to cover the factual aspects of human rights legislation in the UK.

- *Is the learner a victim of torture?*
  The learner may need additional support, as offered by the Medical Foundation or the Refugee Council. See the Resources section, p. 69.

Community involvement

- *How long has the learner been in the UK?*
  If the learner has just arrived, this section is not the first priority.

- *Does the learner attend a place of worship locally?*

- *Does the learner have school-age children?*
  If they have been here some time, the learner may be already
  engaged in active citizenship. For example, helping in their child's
  school, acting as an interpreter for family and friends at the doctors,
  helping at their place of worship, running a youth group or
  supplementary school.

Many ESOL providers are now running ESOL and citizenship courses,
developed in response to the new legislation and to meet learners'
needs. The case studies below are examples of combining models of
provision.

Case studies

CASE STUDY: CITIZENSHIP COURSES AT LEICESTER COLLEGE

1. Embedded citizenship

The vast majority of our provision at Entry Levels and above now
includes an element of embedded citizenship, which is clearly
detailed in the schemes of work. Teachers are encouraged to use
the materials pack and other source materials, as well as realia,
visits and guest speakers to supplement the materials and to make
citizenship as relevant as possible to the particular group of
learners.

2. Preparation courses for the Life in the UK Test

The College also offers short courses aimed at preparing students
at Entry 3 or above who wish to sit the *Life in the UK* test. These
classes consist of discussion of the issues described in the relevant
chapters of the source book produced by the Home Office, as well
as use of students' own experience and knowledge. Visits and
guest speakers are also planned to make the course interesting and
relevant.

---

3. ESOL for citizenship courses

These classes are aimed at students who are not ready to follow the Preparation Course for the test because their language level is still identified as being Entry 2. These classes can be used by students applying for naturalisation as evidence that they have attended a course in ESOL with a significant content of citizenship.

CASE STUDY: NORFOLK MUSEUMS AND ARCHAEOLOGY SERVICE – PREPARING FOR CITIZENSHIP IN A HANDS-ON WAY

For the Norfolk Museums and Archaeology Service the citizenship focus has offered an excellent opportunity to extend its work with this target group and to use its collections and sites as an integral and valuable part of the students' learning experience.

Developing citizenship in a museum context was particularly attractive, given that the Norwich museum is filled with displays and artefacts which explore British history and culture.

Norwich Castle Museum and Art Gallery approached the Norfolk Learning Partnership (which is linked to the Learning and Skills Council) and it brokered a partnership between Norwich Castle Museum and Easton College.

The aim was to provide a five-week, hands-on course followed by an extended seven weeks for students who wished to continue. The course itself was co-tutored – by a museum educator and an ESOL tutor. Using *Life in the United Kingdom: A Journey to Citizenship*, the tutors worked together to create a well-coordinated programme in which the historical and cultural aspects developed the students' knowledge and understanding and also extended and developed their language skills.

The five-week course attracted 11 students from a wide range of countries – Vietnam, Pakistan, Kurdistan, Japan, Bangladesh, Sweden and Poland. An initial student assessment was not undertaken, thus resulting in a wide range of language abilities – from Pre-Entry to Level 2. This heightened the challenge for tutors.

The course was characterised by an active approach to learning. Students were able to get their hands on real museum artefacts such as Roman mosaics, Anglo-Saxon stirrups and medieval drinking vessels to help them understand what past migrations to Britain had been like. A growing knowledge of Britain's past heritage developed alongside improving language skills and vice versa. Typically, each session contained a mixture of elements including the handling of authentic, historical artefacts from the museum collections; the visiting of relevant displays within the museum and the development of language skills.

Outcomes

The extended course could enable those ESOL learners at the lower Entry Level to achieve citizenship status through an ESOL and citizenship *Skills for Life* course. This will be an important gain for students.

Also valuable was the active, hands-on approach to learning. This helped to increase the course's impact; it motivated the students and, as they themselves commented, gave them a growing self-confidence in their own ability to learn.

There was also a more subtle benefit – one which reflects an underlying aim of citizenship; namely, to enable new immigrants to become part of their new community. Working in Norwich Castle, one of the city's most prominent buildings, learners were able to become more familiar with their locality. In other circumstances, the museum may not have been a building that they would have felt comfortable to enter and explore; the course created this opportunity. A visit to the local library, in which students were introduced to the library service and became library members, also served to develop the learners' sense of place and community.

Lessons learnt

The pilot taught the new partnership, i.e. the museum and the college, some lessons and there are aspects which will change in the future.

The decision not to provide an initial assessment meant that the range of language levels was too diverse and this had to be carefully managed. It would have been better to make some initial assessment. This would have benefited the students themselves as the Pre-Entry Level students were sometimes disheartened by their relative lack of language skills.

In turn, this mixture of levels had an impact on the feasibility of all students to take the test and the extended course was critical in helping those at the lower levels to work towards an ESOL citizenship course.

Funding

The course was offered free to all students. Not only that, but students were given annual museum passes to encourage them to make return visits. This has been offered in the past for *Skills for Life* courses and has proved a good way of encouraging students to return with their families. Some have even upgraded their pass to a family pass.

The course was funded by the museum, from a small, one-off budget ring-fenced for adult learning, and in particular for *Skills for Life*/ESOL learners, while the cost of the citizenship test was to be met by the Norfolk Learning Partnership.

Faye Kalloniatis

providers to enrich and enhance the learners' overall experience while helping them to satisfy the Home Office language requirements for citizenship. The introduction of new legislation in 2007, extending the language requirement to settlement, means that it is even more important that ESOL practitioners feel confident to deliver ESOL in the context of citizenship.

This book makes a contribution to the information currently available and the resources listed in the next section make a further contribution.

References and resources

These resources will be useful in two ways. The first section is a list of key resources you need relating to the Home Office regulations and citizenship. The second section is a range of resources for learning materials relating to citizenship for ESOL learners.

Home Office regulations and citizenship

Commission for Racial Equality (2005) *Citizenship and Belonging: What Is Britishness?* A CRE research study. At: www.cre.gov.uk/downloads/what_is_britishness.pdf

Department for Education and Skills (2001) *Adult ESOL Core Curriculum.* London: DfES

HM Government (2002) *The Nationality, Immigration and Asylum Act.* The Stationery Office. Available to buy from www.tsoshop.co.uk

Home Office (2001) *Community Cohesion: A Report of the Independent Review Team,* Chaired by Ted Cantle. London: Home Office

Home Office (2003) *The New and the Old.* The report of the Life in the United Kingdom Advisory Group. Available from Home Office Social Policy Unit, 6th floor, Apollo House, Croydon CR6 3RR. Email: imran.khan@homeoffice.gsi.gov.uk

Home Office (2004) *Life in the United Kingdom: A Journey to Citizenship.* London: HMSO. Published on behalf of the Life in the United Kingdom Advisory Group. Available priced at £9.99 from TSO, PO Box 29, Norwich NR3 1GN. Tel: 0870 600 5522. Email: book.orders@tso.co.uk

Home Office (2005) Home Office Immigration and Nationality Directorate, Naturalisation Requirements (updated 7 December 2005). At: http://www.ind.homeoffice.gov.uk/applying/nationality/

Life in the UK test. At: www.lifeintheuktest.gov.uk

LSC (2005) *Delivering Skills for Life. New Regulations on the Processes for Confirming the English Language Ability of Citizenship Applicants: Implications for LSC-funded Providers.* Fact sheet 7 (supersedes fact sheet 5). At: http://readingroom.lsc.gov.uk/lsc/2005/funding/providers/delivering-skills-for-life-factsheet-7-2005.pdf

NIACE and LLU+ (2005) *Citizenship Materials for ESOL Learners.* Leicester: NIACE. At: www.esolcitizenship.org.uk

Osler, A.and Starkey, H. (2005) *Citizenship and Language Learning, International Perspectives.* Stoke-on-Trent: Trentham Books.

QCA (1998) *Education for Citizenship and the Teaching of Democracy in Schools.* Report of the advisory group on citizenship. London: QCA.

Saggar, S. (2006) 'Dividends of diversity', *RSA Journal,* 26 January 2006. At: www.rsa.org.uk/journal

Written ministerial statement (November 2005) *Tests of language and knowledge of life in the UK for new citizens.*

Citizenship for ESOL learners – learning materials

The network for teachers of English in Brazil. See:
www.britishcouncil.org.br/forum/index.php?s=e4dd883366b51b027ac
6741e897b11d2&showtopic=298

Haenlein, C. and Roffey, S. (2005) Living in Britain: Language and
Citizenship Skills for Accessing Information, Help and Advice in the
UK. Charlson Publishers.

Icons: A Portrait of England: *www.icons.org.uk*

There is a multi-faith calendar (www.bbc.co.uk/religion/calendar) on
the BBC website showing religious festivals and celebrations of eight
world faiths. Race for Justice has also produced a calendar of religious
and cultural events (www.r4rj.org.uk/religiouscalendars.htm). The City
of Bradford Metropolitan District Council in partnership with Bradford
District Care Trust, SHAP Working Party and Bradford Social Services
Black Workers Support Group has produced a very useful religious
calendar (www.bradford.gov.uk/life_in_the_community/religion/
religious_calendar.htm). Diversiton has produced its 2006 multi-faith
calendar (www.diversiton.com/downloads) which is free to download
from its website and covers the main feasts, festivals and holy days of
Islam, Buddhism, Christianity, Hunduism, Bahá'í faith, Judaism,
Sikhism, Confucianism, and Zoroastrianism, as well as secular dates.

British pound coins for the learning activity in Chapter 5 are illustrated
on the Royal Mint website: www.royalmint.com/RoyalMint/web/
site/Corporate/Corp_british_coinage/CoinDesign/OnePoundCoin.asp

The SHAP calendar of religious festivals is obtainable from the SHAP
working party by calling 020 7898 1494.

Spartacus Educational is a useful online encyclopaedia dealing mainly
with history. See: www.spartacus.schoolnet.co.uk

Woodland Junior School in Kent has an award-winning website which includes pages on British culture. See: www.woodlands-junior.kent.sch.uk